Begin Again

Path to Peace Month One

A 30-Day Practice of Self-Compassion & Mindful Awareness

A LostBreeze production

Rediscover the world through fresh eyes and gentle awareness.

This journal includes mindfulness prompts and optional physical practices such as stretching, breathwork, grounding, and cold exposure. While these practices are generally safe for most people, please use your best judgment and always consult a qualified healthcare provider before beginning any new physical or mental health routine—especially if you have preexisting conditions.
This journal is not a replacement for medical advice, therapy, or emergency care.
Your well-being is important. Stay safe, and listen to your body.

Dedicated to the newbies, first timers, apprentices and novices.

Welcome
to the Path to Peace series

Journaling is one of the most powerful tools we have for understanding ourselves.
When combined with mindfulness, it becomes something even deeper:
a practice of meeting each moment with curiosity, compassion, and acceptance.
This series is designed to guide you through six essential aspects of mindfulness.

Begin Again
Approaching each experience as if for the first time

Releasing Verdicts
Letting go of labels and criticism

In the Waiting
Allowing your life to unfold in its own time

Comforting Fall
Believing in your capacity to grow and heal

Space Between
Releasing the constant urge to improve

All That Remains
Embracing yourself and your life as they are

Each of these qualities supports the others.
Together, they create a foundation for greater peace, resilience, and self understanding.
This is not the only way to practice mindfulness.
It is simply one path among many—
a gentle companion for anyone who wants to walk more kindly with themselves.
You are free to adapt, skip, or revisit any part of this journal.
There is no right or wrong way to begin.
Wherever you start is exactly the right place.

Welcome to
Begin Again

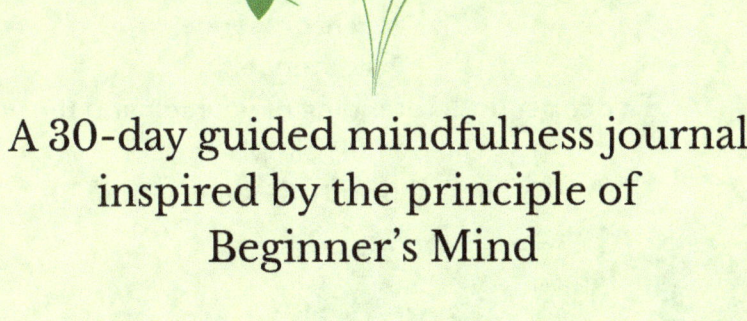

A 30-day guided mindfulness journal
inspired by the principle of
Beginner's Mind

What is Beginner's Mind, you might ask?

It's the willful act of viewing the world through fresh, unbiased eyes—an intentional return to wonder and openness.
In the hustle and busyness of daily life, we often overlook the beauty around us, take kindness for granted, or fall into the belief that we already know all there is to know.
This journal invites you to gently challenge that.
Whether you're feeling stuck, overwhelmed, or simply ready to reawaken your curiosity—these next 30 days are for you.
Try moving through this month with the openness of a child—seeing things as though for the very first time. This doesn't mean being immature or reckless. Instead, imagine waking up with amnesia, where everything feels brand new. Question old rules. Revisit assumptions. Let go of certainty.
And when you think you've "arrived," remember the cellist Pablo Casals. When asked why he still practiced at age 67, he said: "Because I think I am making progress."
The goal isn't perfection.
It never will be.
The goal is presence.
Persistence.
And a deeper understanding of yourself and the world.
The point is simply this:
You showed up—for you.

Although this is Book One in the Path to Peace series, there is no single path you must follow. You don't need to begin here— or anywhere specific.
You begin where you are.
You return when you need.
Each prompt in this journal is paired with a gentle practice something designed to bring the idea off the page and into your breath, your body, your life.
Some will feel natural. Some may not. That's okay.
Try them anyway.
Keep what resonates. Release what doesn't.
This is not a test. It's not a race. And there's no finish line waiting to be crossed.
Growth, peace, and presence are not destinations.
They are ways of being that you may have simply forgotten how to lean into.
You are allowed to miss a day.
To skip a page.
To come back months later.
This journal is a conversation
quiet and curious
between you and yourself.
So move gently.
Stay open.
Let this be a soft return... not to who you were, but to who you're becoming.
Let's begin
again.

Begin Again

What are you hoping to gain from this journey into Beginner's Mind?

Science shows that approaching life with curiosity can rewire your brain toward openness and adaptability. When we intentionally release assumptions, we allow for new neural pathways to form—enhancing creativity, lowering stress, and increasing present-moment awareness. This month is about gently loosening the grip of "I already know" so you can meet life with fresh eyes. Today, begin by asking what you hope will shift or grow in you.

Daily activity

Set a beginner's intention.

Find a quiet space. Take three deep breaths. Then write down one thing you want to be more open to this month— whether it's a habit, a feeling, a relationship, or simply yourself. Place that word or phrase somewhere you'll see it daily: your mirror, your phone lock screen, a sticky note on the fridge. Let it be a gentle reminder to stay curious.

We begin again not because we failed before, but because every moment is a door we've never stepped through.

Begin Again

What assumptions do you carry into your daily life—and how might they quietly shape the way you see the world?

Consider the expectations you bring into your relationships, your work, or even your self-talk. How often do you assume you already know how things will go? Where might those assumptions be dulling your sense of wonder, or keeping you from seeing what's really there?

Daily activity

Walk without assumptions.

Go for a short walk (5–10 minutes), preferably somewhere familiar. As you move, try to notice five things you've never really paid attention to before: textures, sounds, objects, colors. Pretend you've never walked this path before. Let yourself be surprised. Write about what stood out—what shifted when you stepped out of expectation?

Curiosity opens doors we didn't know were closed.

Begin Again

Think of a recent conversation. What might have changed if you had truly listened without preconceptions?

Did you listen to respond, or to understand? Were you waiting for your turn to speak, or did you feel open and curious about what they were really trying to say? Imagine how the exchange might have shifted if you entered it without assumptions—about the person, their intentions, or even your role in the conversation.

Daily activity

Conscious Listening Practice (5–10 min):
Choose one conversation today—big or small—and commit to listening fully. Before the moment arrives, take 3 deep breaths and silently remind yourself:
"I'm here to understand, I'm here to listen."
Focus on their tone, pacing, body language. Afterward, reflect briefly on what you noticed that you might have missed otherwise.

To truly listen is to let go of the need to already know.
That's where connection begins.

Begin Again

Reflect on a time when believing you already knew the answer led you off course.

Cognitive science shows that certainty activates the brain's reward system—but overconfidence often blinds us to alternatives. When we think we already know, we stop listening, stop questioning, and stop evolving. This prompt invites you to revisit a moment where your certainty may have closed doors. By reflecting without judgment, you can learn to soften that reflex and invite curiosity next time.

Daily activity

Rerun the moment—this time with curiosity.

Sit somewhere quiet and replay that memory in your mind. Then, write two versions: what actually happened, and how it might have gone if you had paused and asked a question instead of assuming. Where might things have unfolded with more understanding, grace, or insight?

Wonder often hides in plain sight.

Begin Again

What in your daily routine have you stopped truly seeing?

Familiarity is a quiet eraser. When we repeat the same tasks or tread the same paths, the mind starts to filter them out—labeling them as known, unimportant, done. But there's still life hiding in the ordinary. When you slow down and see something as if for the first time, you invite the world to become vivid again. Awe isn't always about the new—it's about the noticing.

Daily activity

Return to the ordinary.

Choose one habitual part of your day—making coffee, brushing your teeth, folding laundry. Perform it slowly and silently. Notice the textures, scents, sounds. Resist labeling it as boring or routine. Just observe. Afterward, write about how it felt to truly be with it.

Even the well-worn path glows
when seen through eyes that are truly open.

Begin Again

What assumptions do you typically hold about your loved ones?

It's easy to think we know the people closest to us. We predict their reactions, finish their sentences, expect them to stay the same. But love can become dulled by certainty.
When we assume, we stop listening.
When we release those assumptions, we make space for others to evolve—and for deeper connection to unfold.

Daily activity

See someone as if for the first time.

Choose one person in your life and approach a conversation or interaction today with fresh curiosity. Listen without preloading their answers in your head. Afterward, journal what you noticed. Did something surprise you? Did they seem different when seen without the lens of assumption?

Let go of who you think they are
So you can meet who they're becoming

Begin Again

Think of a place you visit often.
What familiar details have faded into the background?

How has that changed from your first memory?
When a place becomes part of your routine, its details blur into the backdrop. What was once vivid becomes assumed—until we pause and return to it with new eyes. Revisiting your early impressions can reveal not only how the place has changed, but how you have, too.

Daily activity

Walk a familiar path with beginner's eyes.

Today, go to a place you know well—your porch, a room, a street—and pause. Stand or sit still for five full minutes. Look around as if it's your very first time there. What surprises you? What feels different when truly seen?

The ordinary hides miracles in plain sight

Congratulations!

That's a full week done.
Seven days where you showed up for
yourself—again and again

(even if you skipped around—no judgment)

Now is a perfect time to pause,
set the journal down,
and simply **BE.**
You're doing amazing work, but rest is part
of that process too. So today, give yourself
that gift of stillness.

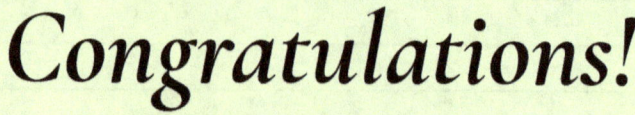

Still Here?

If you're the type who still needs something to do, here's a gentle suggestion:

Try a body scan paired with diaphragmatic breathing.

Find a comfortable place to sit or lie down. Place one hand on your belly and one on your chest. Focus on breathing deeply enough that only your belly rises and falls. Once your breath settles into your diaphragm, bring your attention to the top of your head.

Slowly scan down—crown, forehead, cheeks, jaw, neck, shoulders—all the way to your toes. At each area, observe without judgment. Release tension. Notice any hollowness, tightness, or discomfort.

If you fall asleep mid-way, that's okay. Let it be part of the healing. This is about noticing where you hold tension, where you might be asking too much of yourself without even realizing it.

This technique is used even in military training to help soldiers rest in high-stress environments. You're safe now. Let your body remember that.

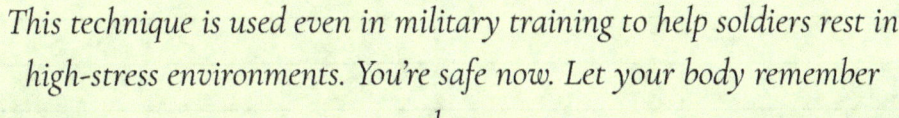

Begin Again

How does it feel to not know something?
What emotions does uncertainty bring up for you?

Uncertainty is often met with discomfort—we rush to solve, explain, or avoid it. But not knowing is also the gateway to wonder. It humbles us, invites curiosity, and stretches the edges of our understanding. The way we meet the unknown shapes our growth. What do you feel when you don't have an answer? Is it fear? Excitement? Something else entirely?

Daily activity

Breathe into uncertainty.

Try a grounding breathwork technique: inhale for 4 counts, hold for 4, exhale for 6. Repeat for 5 minutes. As you do, bring to mind something unresolved in your life—not to fix it, but to sit with it. Let your breath make space for not knowing. Afterward, write what it brought up for you.

Wonder begins where certainty ends

Begin Again

Reflect on a self-limiting belief you hold— perhaps about your abilities, worthiness, or potential.

When did you first adopt this belief?
What experiences or influences reinforced it?
We all carry quiet beliefs that shape how we move through the world. Some of them were never ours to begin with— handed down through childhood, past failures, or careless words. When left unexamined, they can fence off possibility. What belief holds you back, even now? Can you trace its origin? And who might you become if you no longer needed to carry it?

Daily activity

Write a letter to the belief.
Address it directly. Tell it how it has helped you survive, how it has protected or restrained you—and whether you're ready to let it go. You don't need to resolve it today. You just need to begin the conversation. Burn or tear the letter if it feels right.

A belief, once named, begins to loosen its grip.

Begin Again

Tomorrow, how can you intentionally infuse your morning with a spirit of exploration and discovery? What small actions can you take to make the day feel like an exciting journey?

Each new morning carries a quiet invitation: to begin again. To greet the familiar with new eyes. Whether it's the way sunlight hits the kitchen floor or how the air feels on your skin, you can turn routine into ritual with just a shift in awareness. Where could you add curiosity? What if the day ahead were not just a schedule, but an adventure waiting to unfold?

Daily activity

Create a morning micro-ritual.

Before tomorrow begins, choose one intentional act to greet the day: a walk without your phone, a new song while you stretch, a moment at the window with your tea. Something small. Something different. Set the tone for a day seen with fresh eyes.

Everyday is a new beginning

Begin Again

What did your younger self find endlessly fascinating? What happens when you look through their eyes again —right now?

Before you were told what mattered, what was "silly," or what should be left behind, there was a version of you who chased clouds, asked strange questions, and laughed at things no one else noticed. That child isn't gone—they're simply quieted. Can you let them speak today? What might they show you about what still lights you up?

Daily activity

Engage in five minutes of unstructured play.

It doesn't have to be complex—doodle with crayons, build something, spin in a circle, dance poorly, make shadow puppets. Don't do it for anything. Just let yourself explore, without outcome, as you once did.

Your inner child isn't lost
They're just waiting for permission to rejoin

Begin Again

What do you think you know about someone—and what might you be missing?

Every person you meet carries entire galaxies of experience, story, and mystery within them. Yet we often reduce them to fragments: a tone of voice, a style of clothing, a shared label. When was the last time you truly saw someone as if for the first time, free of assumption? Could you?
Reflect on a recent interaction. What silent narratives did you bring with you? What truths might have gone unnoticed beneath your certainty?

Daily activity

Practice silent observation.

Spend five minutes in quiet presence with another person—either in passing or in conversation. Resist the urge to label, define, or judge. Let their existence be enough. If no one is present, look at a photo of a loved one and observe as if you've never seen them before.

Meeting life without labels makes room for truth

Begin Again

**Write about a time you were wrong.
What did it teach you—and how did it change the way you see?**

We often carry shame around being wrong, but mistakes are portals to deeper understanding. When you admit you were wrong, you crack open the shell of certainty—and from that crack, growth emerges. Think back to a moment when you realized your assumption, belief, or judgment didn't hold up. What did that moment reveal? How did it shift your perspective, your relationships, or your humility?

Daily activity

Revisit a belief you once held firmly.

Take 5–10 minutes to reflect on something you used to believe about the world, yourself, or others that you no longer do. Where did it come from? Why did it change? Write a few lines acknowledging the growth it represents. Then, if you're open to it, ask: What belief might shift next?

Mistakes are only negative if we don't learn

Begin Again

What draws you to certainty?
What do you feel in its absence?

Certainty can feel comforting, like solid ground beneath our feet. But have you ever noticed how it also narrows your view, cutting off possibility before it can bloom?
What might it feel like to let go of needing things to be known, defined, or resolved?
Even if just for a moment—what's waiting on the other side of "I don't know"?

Daily activity

Do one thing today without planning the outcome.

Take a short walk with no set route. Let your feet decide the direction. Or, listen to a song you've never heard before without checking the artist or genre. Let yourself explore without labeling or analyzing.

Uncertainty isn't emptiness
It's space that exists before certainty fills it.

Take a moment to recognize the monumental achievement you've just accomplished!

*Fourteen full days of showing up
for you!
That's no small thing.
Whether you journaled every prompt, skipped a few,
scribbled half a thought, or rewrote the entire page—none of
that matters as much as the fact that you stayed present. You
stayed with it. You stayed with you.
So before you rush into what's next, pause here. Let yourself
feel that accomplishment.
You've earned it.*

Rest & Reconnect

For today, the invitation is simple:
Step away from the inner work for a moment and let your mind breathe.
There's a reason we build in this pause—even your thoughts need time to settle. If
we push too fast through insight after insight, we risk missing the ones that
matter most. Integration takes space.
So here's your practice today:
Go outside.
Find a patch of grass and stand barefoot for five full minutes. Feel the earth
beneath your feet. Let yourself be held.
It might sound mystical, but science backs it: regular contact with the ground has
been shown to reduce stress, lower blood pressure, and help release built-up
inflammation by discharging excess positive ions.
So just like your parents probably said…
Go outside.
Soak it in. Rest your mind. Reclaim your body.
Whatever form that takes today
<u>I'm proud of you!</u>
And you should be too!

Begin Again

When that spark of genuine curiosity ignites, how does your body respond?

Curiosity isn't just a mental experience—it shows up in the body. Research suggests that when we feel curious, the brain releases dopamine, lighting up areas associated with motivation and reward. You might notice a subtle shift: your posture straightens, your breath deepens, or your senses feel more alive.

Today, tune into those moments when something genuinely piques your interest. What does your body do with that spark? How does it help you stay open and engaged?

Daily activity

Practice body scanning during a moment of curiosity.

When something draws your attention—a question, a sound, a moment of wonder—pause and do a quick body scan. Start at your feet and work your way up. What sensations are present? Where do you feel energy, stillness, or warmth?

Your body is a compass of experience.

Begin Again

What opinions or assumptions are you carrying today that might be shaping your experience without you even realizing it?

If you could gently set them aside—just for a moment—how might the world around you feel different? How might you feel different? Would anything become clearer, lighter, or more alive?

Mindfulness invites us to notice what's here without judgment or preconception. Often, we move through our day wearing invisible lenses—stories, labels, expectations—that quietly color everything we see. This practice isn't about fixing or removing them forever; it's about noticing they're there, and experimenting with what it feels like to loosen your grip on them. Even briefly. Even kindly.

Daily activity

Do a 5-minute "label-less walk."

Go for a short walk (outside or indoors) and try to notice things without naming them. Don't call the tree a tree. Don't judge the weather. Just observe. Let each sight, sound, and sensation meet you freshly—without the need to explain or define.

Peace grows where opinions rest.

Begin Again

Imagine viewing your routines, relationships, and responsibilities through the eyes of a child—free from adult assumptions and expectations.

What might suddenly seem magical? What might feel heavy or strange? What would stand out as truly important, surprising, or even unnecessary?

Children don't rush to label, define, or control. They live closer to the raw edge of experience—where things are new, vivid, and full of wonder. Returning to this perspective isn't about becoming childish, but about softening the filters we've inherited. What might your world look like today if you let go of "should" and stepped into could?

Daily activity

Revisit something familiar—but playfully.

Choose a routine task (like brushing your teeth, making coffee, or folding clothes), and approach it with curiosity. Let go of efficiency. Use your non-dominant hand. Sing while you do it. Explore it as if you've never done it before.

Wonder waits beneath the layers of knowing.
Strip them gently, and the world begins to glow.

Begin Again

Describe the last time you experienced genuine surprise.

Was it joyful or jarring? Fleeting or profound? How did the unexpectedness of that moment ripple through your body, your breath, your thoughts?

Surprise jolts us out of autopilot. Whether welcome or unwelcome, it cuts through our expectations and reminds us that the world is not always as we imagine. In that sliver of uncertainty, we often glimpse something real—our reflexes, our beliefs, our capacity to adapt. What did this surprise show you?

Daily activity

Take a "different path" today

This could be a literal path—walk a new route, take a different seat, or rearrange your space—or a symbolic one: order a different drink, start a new conversation, or try a task a new way. Invite surprise, gently. Observe how you respond to the unfamiliar.

Surprise is the breath of discovery.

Begin Again

What Truth Feels Too Heavy to Set Down?
And what if letting go didn't mean being wrong?

Certainty often masquerades as safety. It roots us, steadies us, makes the world feel predictable. But sometimes, what we call truth is just a tightly held belief—wrapped around our hearts like armor.

In yogic tradition, the hips are thought to store emotions—grief, fear, and control. When we cling tightly to what we "know," the body clings too.

The jaw locks. The chest tightens. The hips resist.

Beginner's mind invites us to loosen our grip—to meet the moment as if we've never been here before.

To ask: What might I discover if I weren't so sure?

Daily activity

Try a gentle hip-opening yoga sequence or seated twist

The hips are said to store emotional tension; softening them through movement can ease both physical and mental rigidity. Breathe deeply through each posture, noticing what arises when you gently stretch into discomfort without forcing change.

Clarity often comes not from focus, but from perspective

Begin Again

What was your favorite 'why'?

Think back to one of your earliest curiosities—something you asked again and again. Why is the sky blue? Why do people cry? Why do we dream?
Let that moment surface: where were you? Who did you ask? What did you feel when you heard the answer? And—did you ever stop wondering?
Modern psychology suggests that revisiting childhood questions isn't mere nostalgia—it's a doorway to cognitive flexibility. By rekindling the spirit of curiosity we once held so naturally, we soften fixed beliefs and invite deeper creative thinking. This isn't regression—it's return.

Daily activity

Take a walk and pretend you are five years old again

Look at everything around you—buildings, bugs, trees, sky— and ask "why?" about whatever captures your attention. Don't try to answer it. Just let the question live. If you're feeling bold, say a few of the questions out loud.

Your questions shape your world.

Begin Again

Can you meet yourself without the script?

Beginner's mind isn't forgetting
it's arriving without dragging the past behind you.
Pick a belief you've carried about yourself — something like
"I'm too sensitive"
or
"I overthink everything."
Now imagine meeting yourself without that thought.
What opens up? Who are you without that old story?
Psychologists say our self-beliefs act like filters, shaping what
we see and how we respond. Stepping outside them — even
briefly — can build the flexibility needed for growth.

Daily activity

New Trick

Spend 20-30 minutes today learning a completely new, low-stakes skill that you have no experience with (e.g., trying to juggle three balls, learning a few words in a completely unfamiliar language, attempting a simple origami fold, or sketching a new object). Focus entirely on the process of learning and the feeling of not knowing, without any pressure to excel.

Humility is a doorway to freedom.

Dear reader,
You've crossed into the realm of habit formation.
That's 21 days—
21 moments you chose to show up for yourself.
21 chances to look inward with curiosity.
21 expressions of self-love, even if some were small or
messy.
That's no small thing. Whether it took 21 days or 21
weeks, you did it—and that's worth celebrating.
Now, if you're the type who still insists on doing
something (instead of resting, which your nervous
system would absolutely appreciate), today's
invitation is one of my personal favorites:

The ICE BATH

Here's the deal:

Fill a tub or basin with cold water and ice
Submerge yourself up to your neck
(or go as far as feels right)
Set a timer for 3 minutes
(Always speak to your doctor before trying extreme exposure therapy like this)
Bonus challenge: try to sway or gently rock the entire time

(If you know you know)

Not feeling it? A cold shower is a great alternative. And yes, the gas station ice bags are fair game if your freezer's looking sparse.
Why do this? Cold exposure has been shown to:
Boost immune function
Lower blood pressure
Increase resilience to stress
Provide a massive clarity boost when your mind feels foggy
Whatever you choose—stillness or freezing intensity—do it with intention. You've come this far. Let it mean something.

Begin Again

What parts of your life have gone numb from overfamiliarity?

Not because they lack meaning, but because you've looked at them the same way for too long.

What person, place, or routine have you stopped truly seeing? Where has assumption dulled wonder?

Choose one — and ask: what would it take to meet this with fresh eyes again? What could your renewed attention restore? Psychologically, repetition breeds cognitive blindness — we filter out what we assume we already know. But attention is alchemy: it brings the unseen back to life.

Daily activity

Do something the "wrong" way—on purpose.
Draw a simple object (your hand, your mug, your pet) with your non-dominant hand. No fixing. No judgment. Just observe.
Let it be messy. Let it be strange. Let it surprise you.
Notice how your mind wants to correct. Notice how your body responds.
Can you stay curious, even when it feels awkward?

There is a world of insight in the pause between moments.
Learn to linger there.

Begin Again

How do you react when you don't know the answer?

When uncertainty arises, what unfolds in you? Do your thoughts race? Do your shoulders tighten? Do you find yourself scrambling for control — or shutting down to avoid discomfort?

What is the story you've come to believe about not knowing — and is it really yours?

Could this in-between space be not a void, but a beginning? Psychologically, our brains crave prediction because it feels safe. But research in cognitive flexibility suggests that leaning into uncertainty — without immediate resolution — builds resilience, creativity, and emotional intelligence.

Daily activity

**Try the 5-4-3-2-1 grounding technique.
Identify:**

5 things you can **see**
4 things you can **touch**
3 things you can **hear**
2 things you can **smell**
1 thing you can **taste**

This sensory reset grounds you in the present moment, helping the nervous system feel safe enough to sit with ambiguity rather than react to it.

Not knowing is fertile ground.

Begin Again

What old stories about yourself are you finally willing to question — even if just a little?

Are there beliefs you've carried so long they feel like truth? Quiet, persistent thoughts like "I'm too much" or "I never follow through" may have slipped under the radar of awareness and become part of how you see yourself.

But where did they begin? Who gave you those stories — a parent, a teacher, a moment of pain you've never revisited? Are they true now? Were they ever?

Neuroscience shows us that repeated thoughts — even if untrue — carve deep grooves in the brain, becoming default patterns. But neuroplasticity also reminds us: what's been learned can be unlearned. Old beliefs can be questioned, softened, rewritten. what do those beliefs look like when viewed through a beginners mindset?

Daily activity

Write one limiting story you've believed about yourself

Read it aloud. Notice what arises — tension, sadness, resistance. Then, gently cross it out and write a new possibility underneath it.

You don't need to fully believe the new version yet — you only need to make space for the idea that it could be true.

Only when you stop standing on someone else's ground can you begin to find your own.

Begin Again

How Does Awe Move Through You?
Can you still feel wonder... or has familiarity dulled the edges?

Does awe rise behind your ribs like a tide?
Does it still your breath, loosen your jaw, widen your eyes?
Awe isn't just an emotion—it's a return.
It softens the mind's grip, slows the heart, and opens the senses. Science shows it even reduces inflammation and expands our perception. But long before science, awe was the soul's way of kneeling before the mystery.
Beginner's Mind asks:
What if nothing was ordinary?
When did you last see something familiar...
and feel it as if for the first time?

Daily activity

Step outside or look out a window for 5–10 minutes

Don't look for anything impressive. Let your eyes rest on the ordinary until something small surprises you. Notice what your body does the moment it happens — do you lean in, breathe deeper, smile? Pause. Stay with that feeling just a little longer than usual.

Wonder doesn't need to be found
it only needs to be noticed

Begin Again

What makes you feel most alive?

Not just busy. Not just needed. Alive.
Is it when you move without thinking? When you create without apology? When laughter breaks past your defenses?
Truly living isn't always loud—it can rise in stillness, in tears, in risk, in awe.
Neurologically, these moments light up your brain's reward centers and dissolve the self-focused default mode. But deeper than that, they whisper who you are beneath routine.
So ask yourself: When do you feel like fire—not function?

Daily activity

Whatever you wrote—make space for it today.
Even five minutes.
<u>Even a single breath.</u>

Return to what wakes you up inside. Let your fire be something you actively choose to meet. You are important and deserve the same time and respect as everyone else.

Your soul doesn't ask you to be useful.
Only awake.

Begin Again

What part of you has gone quiet?

What once felt vibrant but now feels far away
creativity, stillness, trust, honesty?
Sometimes, what fades doesn't leave, it hides. Behind tension.
Behind over-efficiency. Behind a smile.
Psychologically, we form inner barriers to protect against
shame, rejection, disappointment. But those walls, once
lifesaving, can become cages.
Ask yourself: What part of me went silent while I wasn't
listening? And what might happen if I invited it to speak again?

Daily activity

Find a quiet place. Gently scan your body

noticing areas of tightness or stillness. Place a hand there.
Breathe. Ask inwardly, "What are you protecting me from?"
and simply listen
without fixing, without judgment.

Openness doesn't mean unguarded
It means unafraid to feel.

Begin Again

When Was the Last Time Stillness Surprised You?

Not the stillness of absence, but the quiet that arrives
when you no longer assume you know what comes next.
Stillness isn't always empty.
Sometimes it's the hush that falls when the mind loosens
its grip
when you stop labeling, stop rushing, stop solving... and
simply notice.
Beginner's Mind invites that kind of pause.
It shows up in the way your breath slows when you watch
a leaf fall. In how your eyes widen when you see something
familiar and realize you never truly looked at it.
Neuroscience shows stillness like this opens perception,
dissolves mental noise, and even shifts how we
experience the boundary of self.
But Beginner's Mind doesn't seek stillness as an outcome.
It arrives as a side effect of presence.
What might bloom if you let this moment be new?

Daily activity

Set aside ten minutes in nature or under the open sky

No music. No agenda. Just notice. Stay long enough for your
mind to slow. If a sense of awe stirs—even subtly—let it
ripple. Let it teach.

You don't always have to chase peace.
Sometimes, it's been waiting for you to stop.

Dear reader,
Over the last 28 opportunities, you've
steadfastly shown up for yourself.
That alone is extraordinary.

As we approach the close of this part of your
journey, I want to thank you
for your trust, your presence, and willingness
to explore these quiet corners of your being.
It's been an honor to be your guide.
Now... go enjoy your rest day.
You've earned it.

(But for those of you who are still reading this
instead of resting... yes, **you**. Look to the right.)

Okay, workaholic.

Let's talk.

If you made it this far, chances are rest may not come naturally to you.

So today's invitation is simple:

<u>Rest.</u>

Yup.

That's it.

Do absolutely nothing for 10 minutes.

Stare out the window. Breathe. Lie on the floor. Sit in the sun.

Whatever rest fills you best—go do it.

But before you do, find a mirror.

Look yourself in the eye and say (yes, out loud):

"I love you, and you deserve rest."

Then throw in a kissy face and a wink.

(Yes, seriously. Listen the first time)

Now go. Recharge.

<u>You've done enough for today.</u>

Date: _____

Begin Again

What Might Shift If You Stopped Knowing for Just One Moment?

Beginner's mind isn't about forgetting—
It's about releasing the grip of certainty just long enough to actually see.
The brain is a pattern machine. It labels, predicts, and fills in the blanks.
But wonder lives in the blanks.
Mindfulness interrupts that automatic loop. It hands you back the moment, unfiltered.
So today, choose one small thing—
a task, a conversation, a sunrise—
and meet it with no expectation.
What do you notice when you stop assuming you've seen it all before?

Daily activity

Witness the mundane with the purpose of seeing it new.

Pick one mundane part of your routine—brushing your teeth, making coffee, walking into work—and move through it slowly, with full attention. Notice its texture, shape, and rhythm like a first encounter.

Beginner's mind doesn't erase what you know
it frees you to see it freshly

Begin Again

What have you begun to notice that you didn't before?

Has something subtle shifted? A softened reaction, a pattern breaking, a possibility you didn't see until now?
Beginner's mind doesn't always offer immediate clarity—it offers space. And in that space, awareness quietly blooms.
Neuroscience tells us that attention shapes perception—what we look for, we see more clearly. But only when we're willing to not know for a while.
What feels newly available to you simply because you've been practicing curiosity? What's emerging in the space where assumptions once lived?

Daily activity

Practice an awareness walk.

For 10 minutes, move through your environment (indoors or out) without a destination. Let your senses lead: notice color, texture, movement, sound. Every time your mind categorizes ("that's just a tree"), gently ask, "What else is here?" Let the world reintroduce itself.

The door is always there.
It's the seeing that takes practice.

Begin Again

What did Beginner's Mind mean to you at the start of this journey?

And how has it changed—subtly or profoundly—as you've lived into it?

Were you expecting clarity? Simplicity? Did it feel naïve, or refreshing? Have your assumptions shifted? Have your reactions softened? Did you notice space where once there was certainty?

Psychology tells us that cognitive flexibility—the ability to see from new angles—is a key trait of resilience. Spiritual traditions say wisdom begins not in knowing, but in un-knowing.

What part of Beginner's Mind will you carry forward—not just as a concept, but as a lens? A posture? A way to return to yourself in moments that feel rigid, closed, or stale?

Daily activity

Revisit your very first journal entry from this journey.

Read it slowly. Then write a letter to yourself—from the perspective of who you are now. Let it be honest. Let it honor the change, the effort, the awakening.

You just showed up for yourself 30 times.
Read that again.

Dear Reader,
I genuinely hope this journal has sparked something new in you—opened doors that were long shut, or perhaps gently closed ones that were never meant to be open.
Whatever it stirred, my sincerest wish is that it brought you a little closer to yourself.
As you continue along your journey, take a moment to realize:
You showed up—for you—30 times.
Maybe you did it daily.
Maybe it took two months, or even a year.
Maybe you're just flipping through this at a friend's house, or checking it out in a store before deciding.
Even so, in this moment—you thought of you.
You valued you.
I hope you keep doing that.
If you'd like to be part of the conversation, hear about upcoming series, or simply receive a free daily prompt —scan the QR code on the back and join us on social media.
We'd truly love to hear from you.
With care,
—The LostBreeze Team